The Quatrains of Omar Khayyam

Translated from the Persian by Joobin Bekhrad

Copyright © 2017 Joobin Bekhrad.

All rights reserved. No part of this book may be used or reproduced by any means, graphic, electronic, or mechanical, including photocopying, recording, taping or by any information storage retrieval system without the written permission of the author except in the case of brief quotations embodied in critical articles and reviews.

Balboa Press books may be ordered through booksellers or by contacting:

Balboa Press
A Division of Hay House
1663 Liberty Drive
Bloomington, IN 47403
www.balboapress.com
1 (877) 407-4847

Because of the dynamic nature of the Internet, any web addresses or links contained in this book may have changed since publication and may no longer be valid. The views expressed in this work are solely those of the author and do not necessarily reflect the views of the publisher, and the publisher hereby disclaims any responsibility for them.

The author of this book does not dispense medical advice or prescribe the use of any technique as a form of treatment for physical, emotional, or medical problems without the advice of a physician, either directly or indirectly. The intent of the author is only to offer information of a general nature to help you in your quest for emotional and spiritual well-being. In the event you use any of the information in this book for yourself, which is your constitutional right, the author and the publisher assume no responsibility for your actions.

Any people depicted in stock imagery provided by Thinkstock are models, and such images are being used for illustrative purposes only. Certain stock imagery © Thinkstock.

Print information available on the last page.

ISBN: 978-1-5043-7488-0 (sc)
ISBN: 978-1-5043-7489-7 (e)

Balboa Press rev. date: 02/15/2017

About the Author

Joobin Bekhrad is the founder and Editor of *REORIENT*, an acclaimed publication about the contemporary arts and culture of the Middle East. He has also contributed to other publications, such as *The Cairo Review of Global Affairs*, *The Economist*, *The Guardian*, *Anthropology of the Middle East*, *Encyclopaedia Iranica*, and *Harper's Bazaar Art Arabia*, been interviewed by news outlets including *Newsweek* and the CBC, and seen his writings republished in a wide variety of languages. In 2015, Joobin was granted an International Award for Art Criticism (IAAC) by London's Royal College of Art. He is also the author of *Coming Down Again*, a novella, as well as a foreword to Mahdi Ehsaei's *Afro-Iran*.

Acknowledgments 3

Translator's Preface 4

A Note on the Translation 5

Introduction by Dr. Sayed Hassan Amin 7

The Quatrains of Omar Khayyam

The Mystery of Creation 10

The Sorrow of Life 18

Destiny 23

The Cycle of Time 28

Whirling Specks of Dust 39

Whatever Shall Be, Shall Be 48

'Tis Nothing 62

Seize the Moment 66

Bibliography 84

Endnotes 85

Acknowledgments

I would like to take this opportunity to express my sincere thanks to a number of exceptional individuals, without whom this book would never have materialised. First and foremost, I am indebted to Tiraneh Tehranchian, my aunt, who took the time to read my initial draft and considerably helped me improve the quality of the translations on many levels. As well, I must thank Dr. Sayed Hassan Amin for believing in my work and providing a fitting introduction to this book. I am also highly grateful to Majeed Beenteha and Hamideh Najafi for their continuous support, encouragement, and kindness, every step of the way.

This book is not only dedicated to the spirit of Omar Khayyam, but also to that of my late grandfather, Nosrat Bekhrad, a lover of Iran who composed a *divan* of Persian poetry, as well as that of my late great-uncle Dr. Mozaffar Bekhrad, a lifelong admirer and scholar of Persian literature, amongst many other things.

Translator's Preface

Although I have long been in awe and admiration of Iran's great medieval poets, Omar Khayyam has always held a special place in my heart. Not only do I hold dear his beautiful, lyrical verses, but also – and perhaps even more so – his philosophies, which have left an indelible mark on my psyche and soul alike. Therefore, it only seemed natural that when choosing my first Persian poems to translate and share with the world, they would be those of Khayyam.

When I first began translating Khayyam's poems, I had no intention of publishing them whatsoever. Rather, after translating a few of my most cherished poems of his (and enjoying the process thoroughly), I decided that it might be interesting and worthwhile to render into English his collection in its entirety. Although Khayyam is one of the best-known Persian poets in the West, whose work has been translated numerous times into English, I am nonetheless presenting English-speaking audiences with another version of his quatrains to be enjoyed in its own right.

In translating the poetry of Omar Khayyam, I have striven my utmost to stay true to the exact meaning of each word and stanza, while still retaining the rhyme, grace, and spirit of the original Persian poems.

Ultimately, I hope that through this approach, my translation will offer English readers of Khayyam something unique and valuable, as well as do the sage's poetry the justice it so rightfully deserves.

May both Khayyam and the reader be pleased with my humble efforts.

Joobin Bekhrad
London, 2012

A Note on the Translation

The Collection

Unlike other classical Persian poets such as Rumi, Hafez, and Sa'di, whose body of work is largely undisputed, and, for the most part, exists in only one form, such is not the case with Omar Khayyam. To date, many of his poems, although common in sentiment and style, exist in different variations. As well, many of those thought to have originally been written by the man himself are now by scholars considered more likely to have been *attributed* to him. Taking all of this into account, one can imagine the difficulties faced by any translator of Khayyam in choosing a collection of poems to base their renditions on.

The poems presented in this collection are those selected by the great twentieth century Iranian writer Sadegh Hedayat, who published them in his book *Taraneh-haye Khayyam* (*The Songs of Khayyam,* 1934). This collection is reputed amongst Persian speakers and scholars of Persian literature to be amongst the most, if not the most credible of Khayyam's poems.

The Poems

In translating Khayyam's poems into English, I have endeavoured my utmost to stay true to the original rhyme and structure of the originals, which were composed in the *robaii* style. This style of quatrains, utilised by myriad Persian poets, is characterised by the rhyme structure AABA, with the first two and the last stanzas rhyming. While in some cases the third stanza also rhymes, it is not necessary for it to do so. The majority of the translations provided here follow the original rhyme pattern, although in certain cases the AABB structure has been opted for in order to maintain a form and rhyme without compromising the original meaning of the poems.

In addition, the reader will notice that an asterisk has been placed beside certain poems. Hedayat in his collection placed asterisks beside those poems he felt were more likely to have been attributed to Khayyam, rather than written by him. As well, Hedayat chose to group poems of a similar sentiment and nature into eight different chapters. In using his collection as the basis for these translations, I have done the same in both instances, following the exact format and sequence of his book.

Introduction

Dr. Sayed Hassan Amin
PhD (Glasgow), Advocate (Edinburgh),
Attorney at Law (Tehran)
Former Professor of Law at Glasgow Caledonian University
Visiting Professor of Law at Beijing Foreign Studies University

It is a pleasure for me to write this concise introduction regarding the *Robaiyat* of Omar Khayyam for my learned friend, Joobin Bekhrad. As is obvious to most readers of such texts, Omar Khayyam was a great Persian poet, astronomer, and mathematician of the early Seljuk period (eleventh and twelfth centuries A.D.) in Iran.

Omar Khayyam is best remembered for his collection of quatrains, known as the *Robaiyat of Omar Khayyam*. This remarkable literary work owes its fame in the Western world primarily to the first English rendition by the poet and Orientalist, Edward FitzGerald, who brilliantly adapted it in 1859. Not only did FitzGerald render Khayyam's poetry into Victorian verse, but also expertly chose, combined, and arranged a series of his quatrains in such a way that brought about a continuity of thought absent from Khayyam's original work.

Omar Khayyam was born in Neyshapur, a city in the northeastern Iranian province of Khorasan. Little is known of his early life. A man of great learning, he was highly demanded for his knowledge of science and mathematics. He was appointed as the royal astronomer of the Seljuk court, as well as a member of a group of eight scholars chosen by Malik Shah to reform the Muslim calendar.

During his tenure as an astronomer, Khayyam published a series of astronomical tables, known as the *Ziji Malikshahi*, and produced important works on mathematics, including a treatise on algebra entitled *Explanations of the Difficulties in the Postulates of Euclid.* It would not be an understatement to say that his work on algebra was perhaps the most notable contribution of Iran and his age to the study of mathematics. Furthermore, Khayyam was amongst the first to make a scientific attempt to classify equations of the first degree, and consider cubes from the standpoint of the general equation.

After a lifetime of achievements, Omar Khayyam passed away in his hometown of Neyshapur in 1123 A.D., and today his tomb is still frequented by his admirers and followers.

His scientific achievements aside, Omar Khayyam is perhaps best known in the West for his *Robaiyat*. The name is derived from the plural of the Arabic *robaii*, meaning 'four lines' or 'quatrain'. It refers to a literary form consisting of a poem whose first, second, and fourth lines rhyme, and that traditionally follows the pattern AABA.

Simplistic in form, the rhymes of *robaiis* can nonetheless be quite intricate and complex. Triple, quadruple, and even quintuple rhymes are utilised in such poems. The third line is usually, but not always, left unrhymed. Each *robaii* is distinct, and in extant manuscripts, they are placed in an alphabetical arrangement dependent upon the concluding rhyme. In extant Persian scripts, there are around 1,200 *robaiyat* that were formerly attributed to Omar Khayyam. However, no more than around 100 of these are now considered by experts to be authentic.

Essentially, the philosophy of the *Robaiyat* is that man knows only about the beauty and ugliness of this world, and nothing of the hereafter. As God created man as he is, He will not punish him for being as He made him so. Thus, life on earth – the only life of which man is certain – should be enjoyed before it passes into the inevitable unknown of death.

Dr. Sayed Hassan Amin
Tehran, 2012

The Quatrains of Omar Khayyam

رباعیات حکیم عمر خیام

The Mystery of Creation

راز آفرینش

Although a most pleasant appearance have I,
With a tulip-like face, and am as a cypress lithe,
It remains to be known why in the house of dust
The painter of eternity fashioned me thus.

هر چند که رنگ و روی زیباست مرا
چون لاله رخ و چو سرو بالاست مرا
معلوم نشد که در طربخانه خاک
نقاش ازل بهر چه آراست مرا

My coming into being was a forced tribulation,
Only leaving me at life's ways in amazement.
With reluctance have we departed, not knowing
The purpose of this coming, being, and going.

آورد به اضطرارم اول بوجود
جز حیرتم از حیات چیزی نفزود
رفتیم به اکراه و ندانیم چه بود
زین آمدن و بودن و رفتن مقصود

Of my coming, no benefit to the firmament came,
And in my leaving, no pomp and splendour did it gain;
And from none have my two ears heard
What of this coming and going of mine was the aim.

از آمدنم نبود گردون را سود
وز رفتن من جاه و جلالش نفزود
وز هیچکسی نیز دو گوشم نشنود
کاین آمدن و رفتنم از بهر چه بود

O heart, the mystery is beyond your perception's reach;
As learned as the wise ones you'll never be.
Make a heaven for yourself here, with the chalice and wine,
For whether you'll make it to Heaven or not is unclear.

ای دل تو به ادراک معما نرسی
در نکته زیرکان دانا نرسی
اینجا ز می و جام بهشتی می ساز
کانجا که بهشت است رسی یا نرسی

If the heart the true secret of life did know,
At death the divine mysteries, too, would it know.
Today, if when present you know but naught,
What shall you know when you depart tomorrow?

دل سر حیات اگر کماهی دانست
در مرگ هم اسرار الهی دانست
امروز که با خودی ندانستی هیچ
فردا که ز خود روی چه خواهی دانست

Till when on the oceans shall I bricks lay?
Idolaters and the fire temple I've come to hate.
Khayyam, who said there shall be a Hell?
Who to Hell has been, and from Heaven come again?

تا چند زنم بروی دریاها خشت
بیزار شدم ز بت پرستان و کنشت
خیام که گفت دوزخی خواهد بود
که رفت بدوزخ و که آمد ز بهشت

The secrets of eternity neither you know, nor I;
And of this enigma, neither you speak, nor I.
Behind the curtain there is talk of you and I;
When it falls shall neither you remain, nor I.

اسرار ازل را نه تو دانی و نه من
وین حرف معما نه تو خوانی و نه من
هست از پس پرده گفتگوی من و تو
چون پرده برافتد نه تو مانی و نه من

This sea of existence has from the deep emerged;
Not one has ventured to pierce this pearl.
Each one has given voice to their vexation;
As to what is apparent, none can say for sure.

این بحر وجود بیرون آمده ز نهفت
کس نیست که این گوهر تحقیق بسفت
هر کس سخنی از سر سودا گفته است
زان روی که هست کس نمی داند گفت

The celestial bodies that inhabit the skies
Are objects of wonder for the wise.
Beware – lose not your thread of wisdom,
For thinkers wander far and wide.

اجرام که ساکنان این ایوانند
اسباب تردد خردمندانند
هان تا سر رشته خرد گم نکنی
کانان که مدبرند سرگردانند

This cycle of our coming and going
Is of beginning or end devoid.
None have spoken of the truth of this matter –
Whence do we come and whither do we go?

دوری که در آمدن و رفتن ماست
او را نه نهایت نه بدایت پیداست
کس می نزند دمی درین معنی راست
کاین آمدن از کجا و رفتن بکجاست

When the Keeper fashioned nature this way,
Why did He subject it to death and decay?
If it was good, what was the reason for its undoing?
And if it was not, then who is to blame?

دارنده چو ترکیب طبایع آراست
از بهر چه او فکندش اندر کم و کاست
گر نیک آمد شکستن از بهر چه بود
ور نیک نیامد این صور عیب کراست

Those who the followers of wit and wisdom became,
Amongst the enlightened became their guiding flames[i].
From this dark night to dawn, they did not find their way;
They related a tale, and to sleep fell prey.

آنانکه محیط فضل و آداب شدند
در جمع کمال شمع اصحاب شدند
ره زین شب تاریک نبردند بروز
گفتند فسانه ای و در خواب شدند

Those who have in the past departed, O saghi[ii],
Lie now humbled beneath the dust, O saghi.
Drink thou wine, and from me hear the truth:
All that they've said is but hot air, O saghi.

* آنانکه ز پیش رفته اند ای ساقی
در خاک غرور خفته اند ای ساقی
رو باده خور و حقیقت از من بشنو
باد است هر آنچه گفته اند ای ساقی

Those ignorant ones, who the pearl of meaning pierced,
Spoke of myriad things concerning the firmament's wheel.
They tread in ignorance amongst the secrets of the world;
They first bragged about, and in the end fell asleep.

* آن بیخبران که در معنی سفتند
در چرخ به انواع سخن ها گفتند
آگه چو نگشتند بر اسرار جهان
اول زنخی زدند و آخر خفتند

In the sky above, round the Pleiades rests a cow;
A different one, though, lies beneath the ground[iii].
If you can see, open your eyes to the truth –
Between these two cows see donkeys abound.

گاویست بر آسمان قرین پروین
گاویست دگر نهفته در زیر زمین
گر بینائی چشم حقیقت بگشا
زیر و زبر دو گاو مشتی خر بین

The Sorrow of Life

Today, which for my youth is the time,
As per my desire, I'll spend drinking wine.
Find not fault with me – although 'tis bitter, it is sweet;
It is bitter as it is this life of mine.

امروز که نوبت جوانی من است
می نوشم از آنکه کامرانی من است
عیبم مکنید اگر چه تلخ است خوش است
تلخ است از آنکه زندگانی من است

If my coming were my choice, such a thing I'd forgo;
And if I could choose when to depart, when would I go?
There would be nothing better, than if in this wretched realm,
I did not exist, did not come, and did not have to go.

گر آمدنم بمن بدی نامدمی
ور نیز شدن بمن بدی کی شدمی
به زان نبدی که اندرین دیر خراب
نه آمدمی نه شدمی نه بدمی

From our arrival and departure, what have we to show?
And where is the warp of our being's weft to sew?
Many innocent souls in the firmament's cycle
Burn and become dust – where's the smoke?

از آمدن و رفتن ما سودی کو
وز تار وجود عمر ما پودی کو
در چنبر چرخ جان چندین پاکان
می سوزد و خاک می شود دودی کو

Alas, for in vain did we waste away,
And were reduced to ashes by Heaven's blade.
Rue the day, for in the blink of an eye,
With our desires unfulfilled, we to oblivion fell prey.

افسوس که بی فایده فرسوده شدیم
وز داس سپهر سرنگون سوده شدیم
دردا و ندامتا که تا چشم زدیم
نابوده بکام خویش نابوده شدیم

*Though you've reclined with your sweetheart all your life,
And have relished the fruits of this world all your life,
The end holds naught else but your departure –
'Twas but a dream you'd been seeing all your life.*

* با یار چو آرمیده باشی همه عمر
لذات جهان چشیده باشی همه عمر
هم آخر کار رحلتت خواهد بود
خوابی باشد که دیده باشی همه عمر

*Today, when of joy remains naught save its name;
When no confidante save unaged wine remains;
Hold back not the joyous hand from the wine jug,
When today the hand naught else but the chalice contains.*

اکنون که ز خوشدلی بجز نام نماند
یک همدم پخته جز می خام نماند
دست طرب از ساغر می باز مگیر
امروز که در دست بجز جام نماند

Would that there were a place of rest,
Or to this lengthy road there were an end.
Would that after a hundred thousand years, from within the earth,
Like grass would hope sprout tall again.

ایکاش که جای آرمیدن بودی
یا این ره دور را رسیدن بودی
کاش از پی صد هزار سال از دل خاک
چون سبزه امید بردمیدن بودی

Since what man reaps in this realm of two doors
Other than heartache and sacrifice is no more,
Happy is he who never even drew a breath,
And calm he whom his mother never bore.

چون حاصل آدمی درین جای دو در
جز درد دل و دادن جان نیست دگر
خرم دل آنکه یک نفس زنده نبود
و آسوده کسیکه خود نزاد از مادر

* *The one who Earth and Heaven's wheel designed*
Did much grief to a sorrowful heart assign.
Many a ruby-like lip and musk-laden tress
Under the earth's drum and dust's trickery lie.

* آنکس که زمین و چرخ افالک نهاد
بس داغ که او بر دل غمناک نهاد
بسیار لب چو لعل و زلفین چو مشک
در طبل زمین و حقه خاک نهاد

If my fate were in my hands, as it is in those of God,
I would bid it farewell, and of it discard.
A new one from scratch would I then devise,
Whereby with ease would I attain my heart's desires.

گر بر فلکم دست بدی چون یزدان
برداشتمی من این فلک را ز میان
از نو فلک دگر چنان ساختمی
کازاده بکام دل رسیدی آسان

Destiny

از ازل نوشته

On the tablet have the traces of all beings been;
The pen in endlessly recording good and bad has worn thin.
Whatever necessary was allotted the day eternity came to be;
All of our efforts and sorrows are in vain.

بر لوح نشان بودنی ها بوده است
پیوسته قلم ز نیک و بد فرسوده است
در روز ازل هر آنچه بایست بداد
غم خوردن و کوشیدن ما بیهوده است

Since the span of life and a day can't be shortened or increased,
One mustn't over gain and loss be reduced to grief.
The affairs of you and I, with all our resolve,
Be they even of wax, our hands cannot knead.

چون روزی و عمر بیش و کم نتوان کرد
خود را بکم و بیش دژم نتوان کرد
کار من و تو چنانکه رأی من و تست
از موم بدست خویش هم نتوان کرد

The heavens, which bring naught but sorrow,
Settle not till they've stolen what's ours.
If those who have yet to come only knew
What fortune deals us, they would come no more.

افالک که جز غم نفزایند دگر
ننهند بجا تا نربایند دگر
نا آمدگان اگر بدانند که ما
از دهر چه میکشیم نایند دگر

O thou who art the sum of seven and four[iv],
And on whose account are left in constant furor,
Drink wine, for over a thousand times have I told you thus,
'When you're gone, you're gone – thou shalt return no more'.

ای آنکه نتیجه چهار و هفتی
وز هفت و چهار دایم اندر تفتی
می خور که هزار باره بیشت گفتم
باز آمدنت نیست چو رفتی رفتی

At the time my dust was mixed within the mould,
The calamities that from the earth sprung were manifold.
Better than this it is impossible to be,
Since from that crucible was I thus poured.

* تا خاک مرا بقالب آمیخته اند
بس فتنه که از خاک برانگیخته اند
من بهتر ازین نمی توانم بودن
کز بوته مرا چنین برون ریخته اند

Till when shall we speak of the temple's smoke and light of the mosque?
Till when shall we speak of Heaven's reward and of Hell's loss?
The tablet behold, for upon it has the master of decree
Written of all that in eternity there shall come to be.

* تاکی ز چراغ مسجد و دود کنشت
تاکی ز زیان دوزخ و سود بهشت
رو بر سر لوح بین که استاد قضا
اندر ازل آنچه بودنی بود نوشت

* *O heart, since the truth of this world is all but real,*
Much shall you suffer during this lengthy ordeal.
Resign yourself to fate and make do with pain,
For the quill that has gone won't return for your sake.

* ای دل چو حقیقت جهان هست مجاز
چندین چه بری خواری ازین رنج دراز
تن را به قضا سپار و با درد بساز
کاین رفته قلم ز بهر تو ناید باز

Secretly did the firmament whisper in my heart's ear,
'Knowest thou what fate hath ordained for me?
If my circling about was in my power,
From aimless wandering wouldst I set myself free.'

در گوش دلم گفت فلک پنهانی
حکمی که قضا بود ز من میدانی
در گردش خود اگر مرا دست بدی
خود را برهاندمی ز سرگردانی

Good and bad, which are in man instilled;
Joy and sorrow, within divine fate and our will –
Pin them not to the firmament, for on the way of wisdom
'Tis a thousand times more wretched than you, still.

نیکی و بدی که در نهاد بشر است
شادی و غمی که در قضا و قدر است
با چرخ مکن حواله کاندر ره عقل
چرخ از تو هزار بار بیچاره تر است

The Cycle of Time

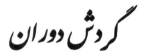

The book of youth has reached its end, alas,
And into winter has that fresh spring of life passed.
This state, to which youth they've given as a name –
We've yet to know when it ended, and when it came.

افسوس که نامه جوانی طی شد
وان تازه بهار زندگانی دی شد
حالی که ورا نام جوانی گفتند
معلوم نشد که او کی آمد کی شد

Alas, our labour's fruits have slipped through our hands,
And on many a bloodied heart does death's foot stand.
No one has come from that realm, such that I may inquire
As to what became of the travellers of this land.

افسوس که سرمایه ز کف بیرون شد
در پای اجل بسی جگرها خون شد
کس نامد از آن جهان که پرسم از وی
کاحوال مسافران دنیا چون شد

For a short while as children did we visit learned men;
As wise ones did we become somewhat happy, then.
Hear now of our fate, and of the story's end:
We emerged like water and became like the wind.

یکچند به کودکی به استاد شدیم
یکچند ز استادی خود شاد شدیم
پایان سخن شنو که ما را چه رسید
چون آب برآمدیم و چون باد شدیم

The congenial companions have all passed away;
One by one beneath death's foot have they been slain.
Our being was but a glass of wine in the ceremony of life;
A short while before us did they to drunkenness fall prey.

یاران موافق همه از دست شدند
در پای اجل یکان یکان پست شدند
بودیم بیک شراب در مجلس عمر
یکدور ز ما پیشترک مست شدند

O wheel of Heaven, destruction comes from your spite;
Your injustice is an old and ancient rite.
And, O earth, were they to cleave your chest asunder,
Would therein be found many a priceless diamond bright.

ای چرخ فلک خرابی از کینه تست
بیدادگری پیشه دیرینه تست
وی خاک اگر سینه تو بشکافند
بس گوهر قیمتی که در سینه تست

Since none wise have profited from Heaven's wheel,
Count the heavens seven or eight, as you feel.
Since we must die and our dreams bid farewell,
What matters if the ant feasts in the grave, or the wolf in the field?

چون چرخ بکام یک خردمند نگشت
خواهی تو فلک هفت شمر خواهی هشت
چون باید مرد و آرزوها همه هشت
چه مور خورد به گور و چه گرگ بدشت

There was a drop of water, and it merged with the sea,
And a handful of dust joined the earth in unity.
What is the meaning of your coming into this world?
Along came a fly – it appeared and disappeared.

یک قطره آب بود و با دریا شد
یک ذره خاک و با زمین یکتا شد
آمد شدن تو اندرین عالم چیست
آمد مگسی پدید و ناپیدا شد

* *'What is this illusory image?' did you once enquire;*
If of its truth I'm to speak, much time do I require.
'Tis an image that appeared from an ocean,
And to its depths then once again retired.

* می پرسیدی که چیست این نقش مجاز
گر بر گویم حقیقتش هست دراز
نقشی است پدید آمده از دریائی
وآنگاه شده بقعر آن دریا باز

'Tis a chalice that the creator of wisdom does fashion,
Who adorns its crown with a hundred kisses of compassion.
Many a fragile chalice does this potter of the universe
Mould, and then on the ground to pieces dash again.

جامی است که عقل آفرین می زندش
صد بوسه ز مهر بر جبین می زندش
این کوزه‌گر دهر چنین جام لطیف
می سازد و باز بر زمین می زندش

The fragments of the chalice moulded as one,
Does the drunkard deem not lawful undone.
Many a precious head, limb, and hand
Were with whose love affixed, and in spite of whom smashed?

اجزای پیاله ای که در هم پیوست
بشکستن آن روا نمی دارد مست
چندین سر و ساق نازنین و کف دست
از مهر که پیوست و به کین که شکست

If the world they lay out for your sake,
Know that those wise nothing of it make;
Many like you come, and many like you go –
Snatch your share before you're snatched away.

عالم اگر از بهر تو می ارایند
مگرای بدان که عاقلان نگرایند
بسیار چو تو روند و بسیار آیند
بربای نصیب خویش کت بربایند

Of those who have departed from this long trail,
Who has returned to relate to us their tale?
Beware at this crossroads, that out of desire
You leave naught behind, for you won't return again.

از جمله رفتگان این راه دراز
باز آمده ای کو که بما گوید راز
هان بر سر این دو راهه از روی نیاز
چیزی نگذاری که نمی آیی باز

Drink wine, for long under the earth shall you sleep;
Without a confidante, friend, or soul-mate sleep.
Beware – divulge to none this secret veiled:
No tulip that has wilted shall bloom again.

می خور که بزیر گل بسی خواهی خفت
بی مونس و بی رفیق و بی همدم و جفت
زنهار بکس مگو تو این راز نهفت
هر لاله که پژمرد نخواهد بشکفت

* An elder did I once see sitting in a tavern;
I asked of him, 'Have you news of those departed?'
He replied, 'Drink wine, for many like you and I
Have gone, and not one has again returned'.

* پیری دیدم بخانه خماری
گفتم نکنی ز رفتگان اخباری
گفتا می خور که همچو ما بسیاری
رفتند و کسی باز نیامد باری

Long have we searched amongst deserts and vales;
Amongst every horizon have we searched and scaled.
Of none have we heard who have come from this path;
The road on which one travels shall one not return to again.

بسیار بگشتیم بگرد در و دشت
اندر همه آفاق بگشتیم بگشت
کس را نشنیدیم که آمد زین راه
راهی که برفت راهرو باز نگشت

Puppets are we, and the firmament our master –
A predicament in truth, not an allegorical matter.
For a short while did we upon this stage play;
One by one in oblivion's chest were we thrown thereafter.

ما لعبتگانیم و فلک لعبت باز
از روی حقیقتی نه از روی مجاز
یکچند درین بساط بازی کردیم
رفتیم بصندوق عدم یک یک باز

O, that we won't be, but the world shall remain;
That we will be gone, and leave no trace or name.
Before this, we were nothing, and after, nothing changed;
Tomorrow, when we've left, shall it still be the same.

ای بس که نباشیم و جهان خواهد بود
نی نام ز ما نه نشان خواهد بود
زین پیش نبودیم و نبد هیچ خلل
زین پس چو نباشیم همان خواهد بود

Atop the earth's carpet do I see ones in slumber;
Beneath the ground do I see those yet covered.
However long I stare into the desert of non-being,
I see those who've yet to come, and those whose days were numbered.

بر مفرش خاک خفتگان می بینم
در زیر زمین نهفتگان می بینم
چندانکه بصحرای عدم می نگرم
ناآمدگان و رفتگان می بینم

This old caravanserai, which the world is called,
Is the tomb of dusk and the particoloured dawn.
'Tis a feast that has forworn a hundred Jamshids;[v]
A grave in which rest a hundred Bahrams.[vi]

این کهنه رباط را که عالم نام است
آرامگه ابلق صبح و شام است
بزمی است که وامانده صد جمشید است
گوریست که خوابگاه صد بهرام است

In that castle, where Bahram held his chalice,
Did the deer bear fawn and the fox recline in peace.
Bahram, who for all his life hunted the onager –
Did you see how by the grave[vii] *he was then seized?*

آن قصر که بهرام درو جام گرفت
آهو بچه کرد و روبه آرام گرفت
بهرام که گور می گرفتی همه عمر
دیدی که چگونه گور بهرام گرفت

I once saw a bird perched atop the temple of Tus[viii],
Which had clutched in its claws the head of Key Kavus[ix].
With the head did it lament aloud, 'Fie upon it, fie!
Where be the jangle of bells and the drum's cry?'

مرغی دیدم نشسته بر باره توس
در چنگ گرفته کله کیکاوس
با کله همی گفت که افسوس افسوس
کو بانگ جرس ها و کجا ناله کوس

On that palace, which once rose to Heaven's lair,
Wherein its court kings displayed a pompous air,
Did we see a dove sitting atop its parapet;
Perched there, it cried out, 'Where, where? Where, where?'[x]

آن قصر که بر چرخ همی زد پهلو
بر درگه او شهان نهادندی رو
دیدیم که بر کنگره اش فاخته ای
بنشسته همی گفت که کوکو کوکو

Whirling Specks of Dust

ذرات گردنده

When our spirits pure leave my body and yours,
Two bricks they'll lay upon my grave and yours.
And then, to make bricks for the graves of the rest,
In a mould shall they toss my dust and yours.

از تن چو برفت جان پاک من و تو
خشتی دو نهند بر مغاک من و تو
وآنگه ز برای خشت گور دگران
در کالبدی کشند خاک من و تو

* *Each speck that has on the earth been,*
Belonged once to sun-faced and Venus-like beauties.
Brush the dust from your sleeve with care,
For it too belonged to the face of a beauty fair.

* هر ذره که بر روی زمینی بوده است
خورشید رخی زهره جبینی بوده است
گرد از رخ آستین به آزرم فشان
کان هم رخ خوب نازنینی بوده است

O sagacious one of old, arise earlier at dawn,
And the child who sifts the dust closely regard.
Give him advice, and tell him to gentle be
With the eye of Parviz[xi] and the head of Key Ghobad.

ای پیر خردمند پگه تر برخیز
وان کودک خاک بیز را بنگر تیز
پندش ده و گو که نرم نرمک می بیز
مغز سر کیقباد و چشم پرویز

How the morn has cleft the flower's skirt, behold;
Of its visage has the nightingale become enamoured.
In its shade recline, for long has this flower
Sprouted from dust, and to dust again returned.

بنگر ز صبا دامن گل چاک شده
بلبل ز جمال گل طربناک شده
در سایه گل نشین که بسیار این گل
از خاک برآمده است و در خاک شده

The clouds billowed and wept over the green grass;
'Tis impossible to live without the rose-tinted draught.
This greenery, on which we loll about today,
Shall whom enjoy when it has sprouted from our ash?

ابر آمد و زار بر سر سبزه گریست
بی باده گلرنگ نمی شاید زیست
این سبزه که امروز تماشاگه ماست
تا سبزه خاک ما تماشاگه کیست

As the New Year's[xii] spring clouds wash the tulip's visage,
Arise, and fill the wine goblets with firm resolve;
For this grass on which you recline today
Shall sprout tomorrow from your ashes tall.

چون ابر به نوروز رخ لاله بشست
برخیز و بجام باده کن عزم درست
کاین سبزه که امروز تماشاگه تست
فردا همه از خاک تو برخواهد رست

Each sprout that has risen by a stream,
Has risen from the lip of an angelic beauty.
Trample not each sprout callously beneath your feet,
For that sprout has risen from the dust of a tulip-faced beauty.

هر سبزه که بر کنار جویی رسته است
گوئی ز لب فرشته خویی رسته است
پا بر سر هر سبزه به خواری ننهی
کان سبزه ز خاک لاله رویی رسته است

Drink wine, for the firmament shall be the death of you and me;
It's laid a claim on the chaste lives of you and me.
On the green grass recline and ruby wine savour,
For long shall this verdure sprout from the dust of you and me.

می خور که فلک بهر هلاک من و تو
قصدی دارد بجان پاک من و تو
در سبزه نشین و می روشن میخور
کاین سبزه بسی دمد ز خاک من و تو

*I once atop an edifice saw a man alone,
Who the mud before him did kick and throw;
And that mire, in its tongue said to him thus,
'Stay put, for like me shall you receive many blows'.

* دیدم بسر عمارتی مردی فرد
کو گل بلگد می زد و خوارش می کرد
وان گل بزبان حال با او می گفت
ساکن که چو من بسی لگد خواهی خورد

Bring forth the chalice and jug, O maiden fine;
Return to the expanse of the verdure by the riverside.
For many a tall moon-faced beauty has this wheel of Heaven
To chalices and jugs demeaned a hundred times.

بردار پیاله و سبو ای دل جو
بر گرد بگرد سبزه زار و لب جو
کاین چرخ بسی قد بتان مهرو
صد بار پیاله کرد و صد بار سبو

Last night did I smash a jug upon a stone;
I was drunk to such a dastardly deed have done.
In a wistful tongue did the jug say to me,
'I was once like you, and like me shall you become'.

بر سنگ زدم دوش سبوی کاشی
سر مست بدم چو کردم این اوباشی
با من بزبان حال می گفت سبو
من چون تو بدم تو نیز چون من باشی

From that jug of wine, which no harm contains,
Fill a bowl, then serve me ten rounds again,
Before the time comes, boy, when we must depart,
And a potter from our dust his pots make.

زان کوزه می که نیست در وی ضرری
پر کن قدحی بخور بمن ده دگری
زان پیشتر ای پسر که در رهگذری
خاک من و تو کوزه کند کوزه گری

* *I passed by a potter, just the other day;*
With dust did he each moment artistry display.
I did see, even if none other heedless saw,
The dust of my father in each potter's palm.

* بر کوزه گری پریر کردم گذری
از خاک همی نمود هر دم هنری
من دیدم اگر ندید هر بی بصری
خاک پدرم در کف هر کوزه گری

* *Behold, potter – if you're watchful, take heed;*
Till when shall you the mud of men demean?
Fereydoon's finger and Key Khosrow's[xiii] *palm*
Have you set on the wheel – what of this deed?

* هان کوزه گرا بپای اگر هشیاری
تا چند کنی بر گل مردم خواری
انگشت فریدون و کف کیخسرو
بر چرخ نهاده ای چه می پنداری

In a potter's workshop did I to myself think;
At the spinning wheel I saw a master sitting.
He made pots sturdy – handles, lids, and all –
From the hands of tramps and the heads of kings.

در کارگه کوزه گری کردم رای
بر پله چرخ دیدم استاد بپای
می کرد دلیر کوزه را دسته و سر
از کله پادشاه و از دست گدای

This jug was once a downcast lover, like me,
Entangled in the locks of a fair beauty.
This handle you see, which on its neck rests,
Is a hand that once a beloved's neck caressed.

این کوزه چو من عاشق زاری بوده است
در بند سر زلف نگاری بوده است
این دسته که بر گردن او می بینی
دستی است که بر گردن یاری بوده است

Last night was I in a potter's workshop;
I saw two thousand pots – some could speak, some could not.
Each one in its present tongue asked of me,
'Where be the maker, buyer, and seller of pots?'

در کارگه کوزه گری بودم دوش
دیدم دو هزار کوزه گویا و خموش
هر یک بزبان حال با من گفتند
کو کوزه گر و کوزه خر و کوزه فروش

Whatever Shall Be, Shall Be

هر چه بادا باد

If I'm drunk on the wine of the Magi^{xiv} – so I am.
If I'm an infidel, fire-worshipper, and idolater – so I am.
Every circle has its own suspicions of me;
I am me – myself is what I am.

گر من ز می مغانه مستم هستم
گر کافر و گبر و بت پرستم هستم
هر طایفه ای بمن گمانی دارد
من زان خودم چنانکه هستم هستم

To drink wine and rejoice – such is my creed;
My religion – freedom from infidelity and belief.
Of the bride of time's dowry did I enquire;
'Your joyous heart', said she, 'is my desire'.

می خوردن و شاد بودن آئین منست
فارغ بودن ز کفر و دین دین منست
گفتم بعروس دهر کابین تو چیست
گفتا دل خرم تو کابین منست

Bereft of pure wine, can I live not;
Without it, this body's weight can I carry not.
I'm a slave to that moment the cup-bearer whispers,
'Have another glass', and I cannot.

من بی می ناب زیستن نتوانم
بی باده کشید بار تن نتوانم
من بنده آن دم که ساقی گوید
یک جام دگر بگیر و من نتوانم

Tonight shall I savour a measure of wine,
And enjoy the riches of two goblets fine.
I'll first divorce thrice[xv] reason and religion,
Then take as my wife the daughter of the vine.

امشب می جام یکمنی خواهم کرد
خود را به دو جام می غنی خواهم کرد
اول سه طلاق عقل و دین خواهم داد
پس دختر رز را بزنی خواهم کرد

* *Upon my death, my ashes scatter far and wide;*
Let my fate to the people be a lesson to guide.
Douse with wine the dust of my body,
And a wretched brick mould from this frame of mine.

* چون مرده شوم خاک مرا گم سازید
احوال مرا عبرت مردم سازید
خاک تن من به باده آغشته کنید
وز کالبدم خشت سر خم سازید

* *Upon my death, bathe my body in wine;*
Words of the purest wine for me recite.
Come Judgment Day, should you search for me,
In the dust of the tavern shall thou this one find.

* چون درگذرم به باده شوئید مرا
تلقین ز شراب ناب گوئید مرا
خواهید بروز حشر یابید مرا
از خاک در میکده جوئید مرا

* May I drink so much wine, such that the aroma of wine
Shall rise forth from the dust, when beneath it I lie.
If perchance atop my grave should a drunkard appear,
From my fragrance of wine shall he become drunk and stupefied.

* چندان بخورم شراب کاین بوی شراب
آید ز تراب چون روم زیر تراب
گر بر سر خاک من رسد مخموری
از بوی شراب من شود مست و خراب

On the day when my life's sapling shall break,
And scattered far and wide shall be my remains,
If from my dust they should mould a chalice,
When with wine they fill it, it shall awake.

روزی که نهال عمر من کنده شود
واجزام ز یکدگر پراکنده شود
گر زانکه صراحئی کنند از گل من
حالی که ز باده پر کنی زنده شود

* *When I am humbled beneath death's foot,*
And extracted from life's hope by the root,
From my dust naught else but a flask contrive,
Such that from wine's aroma I may for a moment revive.

* در پای اجل چو من سر افکنده شوم
وز بیخ امید عمر برکنده شوم
زینهار گلم بجز صراحی نکنید
باشد که ز بوی می دمی زنده شوم

* *When with companions you gather and make merry,*
Your friend must you remember vividly.
When sipping heavenly wine amongst yourselves
And my turn arises, invert your goblets in my memory.

* یاران بموافقت چو دیدار کنید
باید که ز دوست یاد بسیار کنید
چون باده خوشگوار نوشید بهم
نوبت چو بما رسد نگونسار کنید

* Those who slaves to wisdom and purity became,
In yearning for being and non-being naught became.
Go, O knowing one – favour thou the juice of the vine,
For those ignorant became raisins before they were ripe.

* آنانکه اسیر عقل و تمییز شدند
در حسرت هست و نیست ناچیز شدند
رو با خبرا تو آب انگور گزین
کان بی خبران بغوره میویز شدند

* O issuer of the fatwa[xvi], we've more to do than you;
For all our drunkenness, we're more wakeful than you.
You drink the blood of men, while we the blood of grapes;
Be thou just – are we more bloodthirsty, or you?

* ای صاحب فتوی ز تو پرکارتریم
با اینهمه مستی از تو هشیارتریم
تو خون کسان خوری و ما خون رزان
انصاف بده کدام خونخوارتریم

'You're drunk,' a sheikh once to a whore did say,
'Each moment in another trap your foot you lay'.
She replied, 'O sheikh, all you've said of me is true,
But are you in truth that which you display?'

شیخی بزنی فاحشه گفتا مستی
هر لحظه بدام دگری پا بستی
گفتا شیخا هر آنچه گوئی هستم
آیا تو چنانکه می نمائی هستی

* They say that lovers and drunkards are destined for Hell –
'Tis a promise that in the hearts of men sits not well.
Should lovers and drunkards to hellfire be damned,
Heaven tomorrow shall be like an empty hand.

* گویند که دوزخی بود عاشق و مست
قولی است خلاف دل در آن نتوان بست
گر عاشق و مست دوزخی خواهد بود
فردا باشد بهشت همچون کف دست

They say that in Heaven angel-eyed ones reside,
And one can there pure wine and honey find.
If we favoured women and wine, why worry?
Are not our present and hereafter both alike?

گویند بهشت و حور عین خواهد بود
وآنجا می ناب و انگبین خواهد بود
گر ما می و معشوقه گزیدیم چه باک
آخر نه بعاقبت همین خواهد بود

* They say there shall Heaven, houris[xvii], and Kowsar[xviii] be;
A river of wine, milk, honey, and sugar be.
Fill the bowl of wine, and hand it to me –
Better than a thousand promises is currency.

* گویند بهشت و حور و کوثر باشد
جوی می و شیر و شهد و شکر باشد
پرکن قدح باده و بر دستم نه
نقدی ز هزار نسیه بهتر باشد

They say the Garden of Eden is with beauties replete;
I say the nectar of the grape is sweet.
Take this currency, and dispose of that credit,
For from afar is pleasant, O brother, the drum's beat.

* گویند بهشت عدن با حور خوش است
من می گویم که آب انگور خوش است
این نقد بگیر و دست از آن نسیه بدار
کاواز دهل برادر از دور خوش است

No one has seen Heaven or Hell, O heart of mine;
Who, say you, has come from that realm, O heart of mine?
Our hopes and fears are pinned to that to which,
Save a name and notion, we can naught else assign.

کس خلد و جحیم را ندیده است ای دل
گویی که از آن جهان رسیده است ای دل
امید و هراس ما بچیزی است کزان
جز نام و نشانی نه پدید است ای دل

* *I know not whether the one who fashioned me so*
Made me amongst those from Heaven, or repugnant Hell below.
A chalice, a sweetheart, and a lute by the plantation's edge –
These three are my cash, and towards Heaven your loan.

* من هیچ ندانم که مرا آنکه سرشت
از اهل بهشت کرد یا دوزخ زشت
جامی و بتی و بربطی بر لب کشت
این هر سه مرا نقد و ترا نسیه بهشت

Since we've no fixed place in this universe wherein to reside,
'Tis a grave sin then, to be without the beloved and wine.
Till when shall I pin my hopes and fears to sages and the past?
Where shall be sages and the past when from the world I retire?

چون نیست مقام ما درین دهر مقیم
پس بی می و معشوق خطایی است عظیم
تاکی ز قدیم و محدث امیدم و بیم
چون من رفتم جهان چه محدث چه قدیم

Since from the first day my coming was not up to me,
And this undesired departure will resolutely come to be,
Arise and fasten your sash, O cup-bearer nimble,
For with wine shall I wash away the world's miseries.

چون آمدنم بمن نبد روز نخست
وین رفتن بی مراد عزمیست درست
برخیز و میان ببند ای ساقی چست
کاندوه جهان بمی فرو خواهم شست

Be it in Baghdad or Balkh when this life ends, 'tis no matter;
Be it with wine sweet or bitter when the chalice fills, 'tis no matter.
Rejoice, for long after you and I have departed shall the moon
Wax and wane, again and again, forever after.

چون عمر بسر رسد چه بغداد چه بلخ
پیمانه چو پرشود چه شیرین و چه تلخ
خوش باش که بعد از من و تو ماه بسی
از سلخ بغره آید از غره بسلخ

* Other than on the path of the tavern mystics, tread not;
Other than wine, song, and the beloved, seek naught.
From the bottom of the bowl, and the spout of the jug,
Drink wine, O sweetheart, and speak nonsense not.

* جز راه قلندران میخانه مپوی
جز باده و جز سماع و جز یار مجوی
بر کف قدح باده و بر دوش سبوی
می نوش کن ای نگار و بیهوده مگوی

* Saghi, far and wide does my sorrow resound;
My drunkenness has now exceeded its bounds.
I'm content with my white mane, for from your wine
Has my old self the spring of a young heart found.

* ساقی غم من بلند آوازه شده است
سرمستی من برون ز اندازه شده است
با موی سپید سرخوشم کز می تو
پیرانه سرم بهار دل تازه شده است

*A flask of ruby-hued wine and verse I seek;
But an ounce of spirit, and half a loaf to eat.
And then, you and I, reclining amidst ruins,
Would happier than a sultan in his splendour be.*

* تنگی می لعل خواهم و دیوانی
سد رمقی باید و نصف نانی
وانگه من و تو نشسته در ویرانی
خوشتر بود آن ز ملکت سلطانی

** The appearance of being and non-being do I know;
The essence of each high and low do I know.
With all my knowledge, may I be ashamed
If I know of something beyond drunkenness for a moment.*

* من ظاهر نیستی و هستی دانم
من باطن هر فراز و پستی دانم
با اینهمه از دانش خود شرمم باد
گر مرتبه ای ورای مستی دانم

To the cup-bearer's grace do I owe of what life remains,
And of this talk of humanity, disloyalty reigns.
Last night's draught not more than a bowlful contains;
I know not how much of life yet remains.

از من رمقی بسعی ساقی مانده است
وز صحبت خلق بی وفایی مانده است
از باده دوشین قدحی بیش نماند
از عمر ندانم که چه باقی مانده است

'Tis Nothing

O ignorant ones, the figure's form is naught,
And this dome of the nine heavens[xix], naught.
Be happy, for in this realm that raises and ruins,
We depend on but a breath – and that too, is naught.

ای بیخبران شکل مجسم هیچ است
وین طارم نه سپهر ارقم هیچ است
خوش باش که در نشیمن کون و فساد
وابسته یک دمیم و آنهم هیچ است

You've seen the world, and all you've seen is naught,
And all that you've said and heard, too, is naught.
You traversed horizons far and wide – 'tis nothing,
And that grovelling in your abode, too, is naught.

دنیا دیدی و هر چه دیدی هیچ است
وآن نیز که گفتی و شنیدی هیچ است
سرتاسر آفاق دویدی هیچ است
وآن نیز که در خانه خزیدی هیچ است

Imagine the world turns the way you wish – what then?
And what then, assuming this book of life has been read?
Suppose you live to be a hundred, as per your heart's desire;
After living for a hundred more years, what then?

دنیا بمراد رانده گیر آخر چه
وین نامه عمر خوانده گیر آخر چه
گیرم که بکام دل بماندی صد سال
صد سال دگر بمانده گیر آخر چه

* Resting atop the grey earth did I see a knave,
Heedless of Islam, infidelity, the world, and faith;
Devoid of God, truth, the Sharia^{xx}, and belief –
Amongst these two worlds, who has been so brave?

* رندی دیدم نشسته بر خنگ زمین
نه کفر و نه اسلام و نه دنیا و نه دین
نی حق نه حقیقت نه شریعت نه یقین
اندر دو جهان کرا بود زهره این

Of this wheel of Heaven, which leaves us amazed,
The lamp of wonder do we have as a taste.
This world's a lantern, and the sun a light;
We're like images that are spinning inside.

این چرخ فلک که ما در او حیرانیم
فانوس خیال از او مثالی دانیم
خورشید چراغ دان و عالم فانوس
ما چون صوریم کاندر او گردانیم

Since save wind in our grasp, of what was remains naught,
Since all that remains of what is, is brokenness and loss,
It's as if all that isn't in this world is here;
Imagine that all that is in this world exists not.

چون نیست ز هر چه هست جز باد بدست
چون هست ز هر چه هست نقصان و شکست
انگار که هست هر چه در عالم نیست
پندار که نیست هر چه در عالم هست

Look – no inclinations in this world have I got,
And what have my life's labours amounted to? Naught.
A burning candle of joy am I, though when sitting, nothing;
Jamshid's chalice[xxi] am I, though when shattered, naught.

بنگر ز جهان چه طرف بر بستم هیچ
وز حاصل عمر چیست در دستم هیچ
شمع طربم ولی چو بنشستم هیچ
من جام جمم ولی چو بشکستم هیچ

Seize the Moment

دم را دریابیم

The realm of infidelity is from faith but a breath away,
And the world of doubt from certainty but a breath away.
Relish thou then this one dear breath,
For 'tis all we have to show for our life's travail.

از منزل کفر تا بدین یک نفس است
وز عالم شک تا به یقین یک نفس است
این یک نفس عزیز را خوش میدار
کز حاصل عمر ما همین یک نفس است

Seek happiness, for but a moment is life;
A Key Ghobad and Jam in every grain of earth reside.
The state of the world and the essence of this life
Are dreams, fancy, and bewitchment, but for a moment's time.

شادی بطلب که حاصل عمر دمی است
هر ذره ز خاک کیقبادی و جمی است
احوال جهان و اصل این عمر که هست
خوابی و خیالی و فریبی و دمی است

For as long as Venus and the moon have in the skies been,
Better than pure wine, none such a thing has seen.
I'm amazed at the affairs of these merchants of wine;
For what they sell, what finer thing can they glean?

تا زهره و مه در آسمان گشته پدید
بهتر ز می ناب کسی هیچ ندید
من در عجبم ز می فروشان کایشان
زین به که فروشند چه خواهند خرید

The moonlight's glow tore the veil of night;
Drink wine – a moment finer one cannot find.
Be happy, and ponder how long the moonlight
Shall one by one above our graves shine.

مهتاب به نور دامن شب بشکافت
می نوش دمی خوشتر از این نتوان یافت
خوش باش و بیندیش که مهتاب بسی
اندر سر گور یک بیک خواهد تافت

Since none can ascertain the coming of tomorrow,
Be happy, and with joy fill this heart full of sorrow.
Drink wine beneath the moonlight, O maiden, for the moon
Shall go round and round, yet find us not below.

چون عهده نمی شود کسی فردا را
حالی خوش کن تو این دل سودا را
می نوش به ماهتاب ای ماه که ماه
بسیار بگردد و نیابد ما را

How swiftly does this caravan of life pass;
Seek thou the moment that with joy does lapse.
Saghi, why lament tomorrow's misfortunes today?
Bring forth the chalice, for the night shall pass.

این قافله عمر عجب می گذرد
دریاب دمی که با طرب می گذرد
ساقی غم فردای حریفان چه خوری
پیش آر پیاله را که شب می گذرد

At the time of dawn, the rooster of the morn
Crows with despair – know you why it mourns?
It means to show, in the mirror of dawn,
That a night of life has passed, and yet you know this not.

هنگام سپیده دم خروس سحری
دانی که چرا همی کند نوحه گری
یعنی که نمودند در آیینه صبح
کز عمر شبی گذشت و تو بی خبری

'Tis morning – arise, O paragon of charm;
Drink wine, sip by sip, and strike the harp.
For not a soul shall remain amongst those present,
And those who have departed shall not return.

وقت سحر است خیز ای مایه ناز
نرمک نرمک باده خور و چنگ نواز
کان ها که بجایند نپایند کسی
وآن ها که شدند کس نمی آید باز

In our morning revelry, O graceful damsel fine,
Compose a ballad, and bring forth the wine;
For to dust a hundred thousand Jams and Kays[xxii]
Have summer's coming and winter's passing resigned.

هنگام صبوح ای صنم فرخ پی
بر ساز ترانه ای و پیش آور می
کافکند بخاک صد هزاران جم و کی
این آمدن تیرمه و رفتن دی

'Tis morning – let us drink from the rose-hued wine,
And on a stone smash this glass of shame and pride.
Let us quit chasing our lofty hopes and dreams,
And rather clutch flowing tresses and harp strings strike.

صبح است دمی بر می گلرنگ زنیم
وین شیشه نام و ننگ بر سنگ زنیم
دست از امل دراز خود باز کشیم
در زلف دراز و دامن چنگ زنیم

'Tis a most pleasant day – neither hot, nor cold,
With the cloud washing all from the face of the orchard.
The nightingale, in Pahlavi[xxiii], to the yellow flower turns,
And shouts in delight that wine must be poured.

روزیست خوش و هوا نه گرم است و نه سرد
ابر از رخ گلزار همی شوید گرد
بلبل بزبان پهلوی با گل زرد
فریاد همی زند که می باید خورد

'Tis the season of flowers by the field, by the riverside,
With two or three angelic sweethearts aside.
Bring forth the bowl, for the wine drinkers of the morn
Are at ease without the mosque, and far from Paradise.

فصل گل و طرف جویبار و لب کشت
با یک دو سه تازه دلبری حور سرشت
پیش آر قدح که باده نوشان صبوح
آسوده ز مسجدند و فارغ ز بهشت

Upon the flower's visage is the New Year's breeze sweet;
On the verdant green is the beloved's face sweet.
Winter has passed – your words are not pleasant;
Be merry and speak not of winter, for today is sweet.

بر چهره گل نسیم نوروز خوش است
در صحن چمن روی دلفروز خوش است
از دی که گذشت هر چه گویی خوش نیست
خوش باش و ز دی مگو که امروز خوش است

Saghi, how joyful are the flowers and the grass;
Know that next week into dust shall they pass.
Drink wine and a flower pick, for before you know,
Shall the flower turn to dust, and to dust the grass.

ساقی گل و سبزه بس طربناک شده است
دریاب که هفته دگر خاک شده است
می نوش و گلی بچین که تا در نگری
گل خاک شده است و سبزه خاشاک شده است

Like a tulip in springtime, seize the bowl of wine,
With a tulip-faced beauty, should the chance arise.
Drink wine and enjoy it, for this azure wheel
Shall like dust lay you low, all in no time.

چون لاله به نوروز قدح گیر بدست
با لاله رخی اگر ترا فرصت هست
می نوش به خرمی که این چرخ کبود
ناگاه ترا چو خاک گرداند پست

* Each time the violet dons its colourful clothes,
When the morning breeze caresses the rose,
Wise is the one, who with a pretty youth
Drinks wine, and the chalice smashes on a stone.

* هر گه که بنفشه جامه در رنگ زند
در دامن گل باد صبا چنگ زند
هشیار کسی بود که با سیمبری
می نوشد و جام باده بر سنگ زند

Arise, and feel no sorrow for this fleeting world;
Be happy, and for a moment rejoice in mirth.
If the nature of the world did fidelity possess,
Your turn would not come, as it did for the rest.

برخیز و مخور غم جهان گذران
خوش باش و دمی به شادمانی گذران
در طبع جهان اگر وفائی بودی
نوبت بتو خود نیامدی از دگران

In Heaven's sphere, whose depth we do not know,
Drink wine and make merry, for round the wine goes.
When your turn arises, heave thou not a sigh;
'Tis a chalice that all must sip from in time.

در دایره سپهر ناپیدا غور
می نوش به خوشدلی که دور است بجور
نوبت چو بدور تو رسد آه مکن
جامی است که جمله را چشانند بدور

'Tis better from the study of science to flee,
And instead clutch the tresses of a fair beauty.
Before the hour when time shall spill your blood,
'Tis better to spill in the chalice the blood of the jug.

از درس علوم جمله بگریزی به
واندر سر زلف دلبر آویزی به
زان پیش که روزگار خونت ریزد
تو خون قنینه در قدح ریزی به

The days of time do reproach the fellow
Who sits and ponders the world's misery in sorrow.
Drink wine from the chalice, to the cry of the harp,
Before the chalice is smashed upon a stone.

ایام زمانه از کسی دارد ننگ
کو در غم ایام نشیند دلتنگ
می خور تو در آبگینه با ناله چنگ
زآن پیش که آبگینه آید بر سنگ

With winter's farewell and the coming of springtime
Do the pages of our existence hastily flutter by.
Drink wine and lament not, for has said the sage,
'The world's sorrows are like poison, and their antidote, wine'.

* از آمدن بهار و از رفتن دی
اوراق وجود ما همی گردد طی
می خور مخور اندوه که گفته است حکیم
غم های جهان چو زهر و تریاقش می

Before from the world your name must go,
Drink wine, for from the heart does it banish sorrow.
Unravel a beauty's locks string by string,
Before your thread of life wears thin.

زان پیش که نام تو ز عالم برود
می خور که چو می بدل رسد غم برود
بگشای سر زلف بتی بند ز بند
زان پیش که بند بندت از هم برود

* Come hither, O friend – let us not despair of tomorrow,
And truly relish this life that is but a moment.
Tomorrow, when from this ancient realm we depart,
Shall we be just like those seven thousand years old.

* ای دوست بیا تا غم فردا نخوریم
وین یکدم عمر را غنیمت شمریم
فردا که ازین دیر کهن در گذریم
با هفت هزار سالگان سر بسریم

* Speak not, for you're beneath the brazen heavens;
Drink wine, for you're in a world with pestilence ridden.
Since your beginning and end are nowhere save in dust,
Imagine not that you're atop it, but rather, within.

* تن زن چو بزیر فلک بی باکی
می نوش چو در جهان آفت ناکی
چون اول و آخرت بجز خاکی نیست
انگار که بر خاک نه ای در خاکی

* *Hand me the wine, for my heart's aglow,*
And this fast-fleeting life like quicksilver goes.
Know thou that youth's fire is water;
Beware – the riches of wakefulness are in a doze.[xxiv]

می برکف من نه که دلم در تابست
وین عمر گریز پای چون سیمابست
دریاب که آتش جوانی آبست
هش دار که بیداری دولت خواب است

Drink wine, for life everlasting is this;
The fruit of your youth's labours is this.
'Tis the time of flowers, wine, and merry companions;
Rejoice thou for a moment, for life is this.

می نوش که عمر جاودانی اینست
خود حاصلت از دور جوانی اینست
هنگام گل و مل است و یاران سر مست
خوش باش دمی که زندگانی اینست

Drink wine, for like Mahmoud's[xxv] kingdom is it so,
And to the harp listen, for 'tis like David's[xxvi] tone.
Think not of the coming and going of others;
Rejoice and be happy, for such is the goal.

با باده نشین که ملک محمود اینست
وز چنگ شنو که لحن داود اینست
از آمده و رفته دگر یاد مکن
حالی خوش باش زانکه مقصود اینست

Your today is not within reach of tomorrow,
And your thought of tomorrow contains naught else but sorrow.
Spoil not this moment if your heart is aware,
For what of life yet remains has yet to be known.

امروز ترا دسترس فردا نیست
واندیشه فردات بجز سودا نیست
ضایع مکن این دم ار دلت بیدار است
کاین باقی عمر را بقا پیدا نیست

This world, without the cup-bearer and wine, is naught;
Without the murmur of the Iraqi reed, naught.
However much I ponder the state of this world, I can see
No greater thing than joy – the rest is naught.

* دوران جهان بی می و ساقی هیچ است
بی زمزمه نای عراقی هیچ است
هر چند در احوال جهان می نگرم
حاصل همه عشرت است و باقی هیچ است

Till when shall I remorse over what I have and have not,
And whether I've spent this life in happiness, or have not?
Fill the bowl with wine, for it is not certain
Whether this breath I take shall be my last, or not.

تا کی غم آن خورم که دارم یا نه
وین عمر به خوشدلی گذارم یا نه
پر کن قدح باده که معلومم نیست
کاین دم که فرو برم برآرم یا نه

Until in agreement do we clasp our hands,
We cannot trample sorrow and in merriment dance.
Let us rise and draw a breath before the hour of dawn,
For the dawn shall emerge still, though our breath be gone.

تا دست به اتفاق بر هم نزنیم
پایی ز نشاط بر سر غم نزنیم
خیزیم و دمی زنیم پیش از دم صبح
کاین صبح بسی دمد که ما دم نزنیم

Ravenously to the goblet's brim did I bring these lips of mine,
Such that I would the potion of a long life find.
It pressed its lips to mine and in secret told me thus,
'For to this world you won't return, drink thou wine'.

لب بر لب کوزه بردم از غایت آز
تا زو طلبم واسطه عمر دراز
لب بر لب من نهاد و می گفت براز
می خور که بدین جهان نمی آیی باز

Khayyam, if thou be drunk with wine, be happy.
If thou be resting with a tulip-faced one, be happy.
Since in the end, this world will fade to nothingness,
Be as if you do not exist, and be happy.

خیام اگر ز باده مستی خوش باش
با لاله رخی اگر نشستی خوش باش
چون عاقبت کار جهان نیستی است
انگار که نیستی چو هستی خوش باش

Tomorrow shall I the banner of hypocrisy set aside,
And with white hair, resolve to drink wine.
The draught of life has reached seventy –
If I do not make merry now, then when shall I?

فردا علم نفاق طی خواهم کرد
با موی سپید قصد می خواهم کرد
پیمانه عمر من به هفتاد رسید
این دم نکنم نشاط کی خواهم کرد

Heaven's wheel is an image of our figures frayed;
The Jeyhun[xxvii], of our pure tears wept, a trace.
Hellfire's a spark of our useless toil;
Paradise a peaceful moment that we while away.

گردون نگری ز قد فرسوده ماست
جیحون اثری ز اشک پالوده ماست
دوزخ شرری ز رنج بیهوده ماست
فردوس دمی ز وقت آسوده ماست

Till when shall you spend your life with yourself entranced?
Or ponder the mysteries of being and non-existence?
Drink wine, for there is so much sorrow in this life,
That 'tis better to spend it in slumber or drunkenness.

عمرت تا کی بخود پرستی گذرد
یا در پی نیستی و هستی گذرد
می خور که چنین عمر که غم در پی اوست
آن به که بخواب یا بمستی گذرد

Bibliography

Avery, P., & Heath-Stubbs, J. *The Rubai'yat of Omar Khayyam.* London: Penguin, 1981.

FitzGerald, E., *Rubaiyat of Omar Khayyam.* London: Phoenix Press, 2009.

Hedayat, S., *Taraneh-haye Khayyam.* Tehran: 1934.

Endnotes

---

[i] A likely reference to the story of the 'Companions of the Cave' mentioned in the *Cave Surah* of the Koran.

[ii] Cup-bearer.

[iii] The cow/bull in the sky refers to the Taurus constellation (according to Avery and Heath-Stubbs), and the one beneath the ground to the belief in Islam that Earth rests on the horns of a bull.

[iv] The seven classical planets (i.e. the Sun, the Moon, Mercury, Venus, Mars, Jupiter, and Saturn) and the four elements (Earth, Water, Air, and Fire), according to Avery and Heath-Stubbs.

[v] A legendary king in Iranian mythology.

[vi] Bahram V, an Iranian king of the Sassanid dynasty. His love of hunting onager earned him the name Bahram *Gur* (Bahram of the Onagers).

[vii] In Persian, *gur* means both 'onager' and 'grave'. The crux of this poem is the play on words here.

[viii] A city in Iran's Khorasan province.

[ix] A fabled Iranian king whose exploits were celebrated in Ferdowsi's *Shahnameh* (*Book of Kings*), Iran's national epic.

[x] In this play on words, Khayyam uses the word *koo* in reference to both the Persian for 'where', as well as the literal sound of a dove.

[xi] Persian monarchs extolled by Ferdowsi in his *Shahnameh*.

[xii] A reference to *Norooz* (lit. 'New Day'), the Iranian New Year, which occurs at the time of the Vernal Equinox.

[xiii] Storied monarchs in Iranian mythology and history.

[xiv] Zoroastrian clergymen.

[xv] In Islam, a man can lawfully divorce his wife by repeating the phrase 'I divorce thee' three times.

[xvi] A religious order issued by a Muslim cleric concerning Islamic law.

[xvii] Virgins promised in Islamic Paradise.
[xviii] A fountain in Islamic Paradise.
[xix] The nine spheres of Heaven (i.e. the seven planets, Fixed Stars, and *Primum Mobile*), according to Avery and Heath-Stubbs.
[xx] Islamic law.
[xxi] King Jamshid's legendary chalice, which was said to hold the elixir of immortality as well as afford its bearer psychic powers.
[xxii] A reference to the Iranian kings Jamshid and Key Khosrow.
[xxiii] Middle Persian.
[xxiv] A reference to the Persian belief that one is fortunate when their luck is 'awake'.
[xxv] Mahmoud Ghaznavi, a notable ruler of the Ghaznavid dynasty.
[xxvi] King David of the Abrahamic religions.
[xxvii] The Oxus in Central Asia.

Lightning Source UK Ltd.
Milton Keynes UK
UKOW05f1300300617
304416UK00001B/6/P